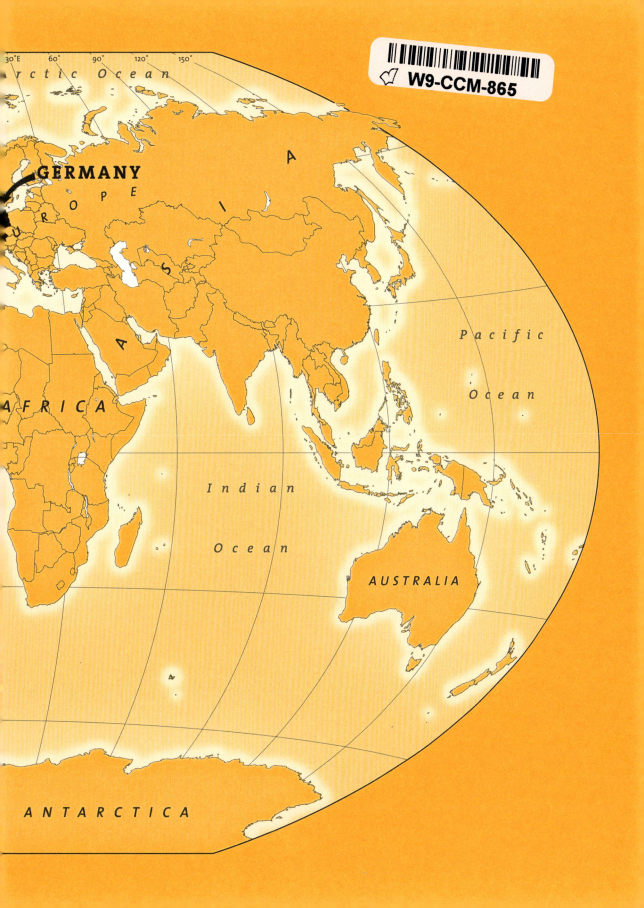

Germany

Henry Russell

Benedict Korf and Antje Schlottmann, Consultants

NATIONAL GEOGRAPHIC

WASHINGTON, D.C.

Contents

Foreword

When Germany hosted the soccer World Cup Finals in 2006, people from all over the world came to visit. After the games, many of the visitors returned to their home country with a completely new impression of what Germany and the Germans are really like. How come so many sensible grown-up people had been mistaken?

There are always certain images at work when we deal with things and people we do not actually know. We use these images to make the complicated world easier to understand, so they are often quite simple. Ask yourself: "What is the typical German like?" You might have an idea that he or she would come across as being efficient and precise, but also a bit square and hung up in contrast to, say, an easy-going Italian. In the same way, most people's picture of Germany is usually a peculiar mix of sausages, Porsches, the Berlin Wall, and Beethoven, in contrast to, say, burgers, Chevrolets, Babe Ruth, and the White House in the United States.

It would be wrong to say that these images are all false. Some of them have a little truth. But the important thing is that they do not fit for all people living in a country at any time and in any situation. That's why our simple images will never match the reality we actually experience. But it's important to remember that there is nothing inevitable about such images. They do not always stay the same, like the law of gravity or the color of the sky. You can change them by reading and traveling, so that you can create for yourself a far more comprehensive picture.

So here you go! Carry on reading this book and you will learn that many people living in Germany are not Germans at all, that there are long sandy beaches as well as great urban centers, and a history that is full of

harrowing downs and memorable ups. In short, I hope that you will agree that there is much more to Germany than its image gives away.

▲ Trams and motor
traffic light up a square
in the heart of Berlin, the
German capital, in a
photograph taken over a
period of minutes.

Antje Schlottmann
Friedrich-Schiller-Universität
Jena, Germany

Between Two Extremes

THE HIGHEST MOUNTAIN in Germany, the Zugspitze, stands on the southern border with Austria. Germany has a number of wild places like this, and even the most remote are easy to get to. The Zugspitze is no exception. Its steep slopes may be covered in snow all year and prone to deadly avalanches, but it is easy to reach the peak. A railroad carries visitors up there, traveling through tunnels carved into the mountain. From the top you can see four countries, south across Austria to Switzerland and Italy. To the north, Germany gradually flattens out into hills and then a wide plain that stretches to the North Sea. Between its two extremes of rugged mountains and flat coastline, Germany is a country of incredible variety.

◀ The Zugspitze is wild and remote, but like most of Germany, it is also accessible: the mountain is home to one of Germany's most popular ski resorts.

At a Glance

WHAT'S THE WEATHER LIKE?

CLIMATE ZONES
Mild
☐ Marine West Coast
High Elevations
☐ Highlands

Germany has a mild climate, but the weather is sometimes unpredictable. Above Germany, warm air from the North Atlantic ocean meets colder air from northeastern Europe. The result is sometimes rapid changes of weather, such as a sudden rain shower on a hot summer's day. Snow falls any time from early November to late April. It may lie on the ground for weeks. The map opposite shows the physical features of Germany. Labels on this map and on similar maps throughout this book identify places pictured in each chapter.

Fast Facts

OFFICIAL NAME: Federal Republic of Germany

FORM OF GOVERNMENT: Federal Republic

CAPITAL: Berlin

POPULATION: 82,422,299

OFFICIAL LANGUAGE: German

MONETARY UNIT: Euro

AREA: 134,838 square miles (349,223 square kilometers)

BORDERING NATIONS: Austria, Belgium, Czech Republic, Denmark, France, Luxembourg, Netherlands, Poland, Switzerland

HIGHEST POINT: Zugspitze 9,721 feet (2,962 meters)

LOWEST POINT: Neuendorf bei Wilster −11.6 feet (−3.5 meters)

MAJOR RIVERS: Danube, Elbe, Main, Rhine

Average Temperature & Rainfall

Average High/Low Temperatures; Yearly Rainfall

BERLIN
55° F (13° C)/41° F (5° C); 23 in (58 cm)

FRANKFURT
55° F (13° C)/41° F (5° C); 22 in (56 cm)

HAMBURG
54° F (12° C)/40° F (4° C); 30 in (76 cm)

KIEL
54° F (12° C)/41° F (5° C); 28 in (71 cm)

LEIPZIG
57° F (14° C)/41° F (5° C); 23 in (60 cm)

MUNICH
55° F (13° C)/38° F (3° C); 32 in (81 cm)

STUTTGART
54° F (12° C)/40° F (4° C); 26 in (67 cm)

DENMARK

SWEDEN

North Frisian Islands

BEACH, page 11

Sylt

Föhr
Amrum

FIELDS, page 10

SHIPYARD, page 13

Baltic Sea

Fehmarn

Rügen

Kiel
Holstein

Rostock

Neuendorf bei Wilster
(Lowest point in Germany)
-11 ft, -3.5 m

North Sea

East Frisian Islands

Bremerhaven

Hamburg

Elbe

Müritz

N O R T H E R N   E U R O P E A N   P L A I N

Bremen

Ems

Weser

Aller

POLAND

NETHERLANDS

MITTELLAND CANAL

Hanover

BERLIN HAUPTBAHNHOF,
page 14

Berlin

Oder

Rhine

WOODLAND,
page 11

H a r z

Saale

Elbe

Neisse

Duisburg

Ruhr

Düsseldorf

Leipzig

Cologne

Erfurt

BELGIUM

Bonn

G E R M A N Y

Ore Mountains

GUTENFELS CASTLE,
page 13

CANAL,
page 15

CZECH
REPUBLIC

LUXEMBOURG

Moselle

Frankfurt

Main

Mainz

RHINE-MAIN-DANUBE
CANAL

Bohemian Forest

Neckar

Danube

BLACK FOREST,
page 12

Black Forest

Stuttgart

Schwäbische Alb

Danube

Munich

Inn

FRANCE

Rhine

ZUGSPITZE,
pages 2, 6-7

Lake
Constance

Zugspitze
(Highest point in Germany)
9,721 ft
2,963 m

Bavarian Alps

A L P S

AUSTRIA

LIECHTENSTEIN

SWITZERLAND

ITALY

MAP KEY

⊛ National capital
● Selected city
+ Elevation
≈ Canal

miles   0 — 100
km   0 — 100

Physical Map

GERMANY

Atlantic
Ocean

Asia

Europe

Africa

▲ Fields of yellow rape (a type of turnip plant) and green grass cover plains in Holstein, the northern most region of Germany. Crops in the north tend to be grown for animal feed; food crops are grown in more fertile soil farther south.

At the Center

Germany's position at the heart of Europe has shaped its history both for good and ill. It borders nine neighbors—more than any other European country. Germany has frequently gone to war with its neighbors, but in the late 20th century, it also led efforts to create a peaceful union of European countries. Germany is not the largest nation in Europe. With more than 82 million inhabitants, however, it has the biggest population except for Russia, which extends east from Europe through Asia to the Pacific Ocean.

Wide Open Spaces

A great plain covers much of northern Germany. It is bounded to the north and northwest by the Baltic Sea and the North Sea. The coast has important ports and some of the world's longest sandy beaches. To the east, the plain extends across Poland as far as the Ural Mountains of Russia.

Northern Germany is not entirely flat. The Harz mountains in the center of northern Germany are cloaked in an old evergreen forest. In German tradition, the forest is dark and magical. It is the setting for many folktales. Every April, witches were said to gather at night on its highest peak, the Brocken.

▲ In addition to gnarled forests, the Harz mountains are also known for spring water.

THE FRISIAN ISLANDS

The Frisian Islands lie in the North Sea, just off mainland Europe. Some belong to Germany; others are parts of Denmark or the Netherlands. In summer the islands are filled with tourists, who go there for the quiet old villages and the wide sandy beaches. The largest Frisian island is Sylt, where wealthy Germans have vacation homes. The other main islands are Föhr and Amrum. They are less built up and still have many traditional farms that specialize in producing cow's milk, although tourism is also important.

Many of the islanders still speak Frisian. It is a dialect of German, but it sounds very much like English.

▲ A long beach on Sylt is covered by small shelters that protect sunbathers from the wind.

Sylt is linked to the mainland by a causeway that carries a railroad. Cars are allowed onto the island, but they have to ride the train to get there. The other islands are reached by ferries.

▲ The Black Forest is shrouded in snow for much of the winter. In the summer, the thick fir trees shut out the light and create the gloomy atmosphere that got the region its name.

Woods and Water

Much of southern Germany is covered in forested hills. The largest wooded area, and one of the most famous, is in the far southwest, near the Swiss border. This is the Black Forest, a mountainous region full of pines and firs. The forest contains the source of the Danube, one the longest rivers in Europe. The Danube flows through central Europe for 1,771 miles (2,850 km) to its mouth on the Black Sea in Romania.

Germany becomes increasingly rugged in the state of Bavaria. Much of the country's southern border runs through the Alps, the tallest mountain range in western Europe.

Riches by the Rivers

Germany's northern plain is crossed by large rivers, including the Oder, Saale, and Main. One of the country's most important rivers is the Rhine. The Rhine rises in two forks in Switzerland before meeting and widening to form Lake Constance. This lake forms the border with Switzerland. The river flows out of the lake again and, turning north, forms the frontier with France, before continuing through western Germany to the Netherlands and the North Sea.

A LEGENDARY RIVER

▲ Gutenfels Castle stands above the Rhine River in western Germany. The Pfalz, an island fortress below the castle, was used to collect tolls from passing barges.

The Rhine is deep and wide and has been carrying traffic for thousands of years. The river has also played a major role in shaping German history: 2,000 years ago the Romans ruled most of Europe, but they found it difficult to cross the Rhine and never conquered the lands to its east and north.

The scenery along the Rhine changes dramatically. On some stretches its banks are lined with factories and great cities. In other parts sheer rocky crags rise high on either side of the river. Dreamlike castles have been built on some of the highest outcrops.

The beauty of the Rhine has inspired legends. The mythical German hero Siegfried is said to have killed a dragon on Drachenfels (Dragon's Rock) near Bonn. A 400-foot (120-m) cliff at St. Goarshausen, near a section of rapids, is supposed to have been the home of Lorelei, a beautiful Rhine maiden who lured sailors to their deaths on the rocks below.

Many of Germany's greatest cities grew up along the banks of the rivers, which were easy to navigate and good for trade. They include Cologne on the Rhine and Frankfurt on the River Main. Germany's seaports, particularly Hamburg, Rostock, and Kiel, are among the busiest in Europe, handling products from around the world.

The biggest and most important German city is the capital, Berlin, which has a population of just under 3.4 million. The next two largest cities are Hamburg, which has 1.7 million inhabitants, and

▼ Cargo ships being constructed in Kiel, the largest German port on the Baltic Sea

Munich, with 1.2 million residents. Nine other cities have more than half a million people.

The Wealth of Nature

The flat land of Germany's river basins is fertile and good for farming. More than half of the nation's land area is used for agriculture. Just under one-third of the country is covered in forest, although much is too mountainous to be useful for logging. About one-tenth is covered in towns and cities.

Germany's many other natural resources include minerals such as iron ore. In the Middle Ages, supplies of iron made the region very wealthy. During the 1800s, iron was the basis of industrial growth and the area's rise to military power. Later, a growing steel

▼ Germany's cities are filled with modern buildings, such as the main railroad station in Berlin. Many of the major buildings have been designed by leading international architects.

industry helped make Germany a leading automobile manufacturer, with brands including BMW (Bavarian Motor Works), Mercedes-Benz, and Volkswagen.

Another natural resource is coal. Germany was one of the world's main coal producers. It has vast reserves of coal, especially around the Ruhr, a river that joins the Rhine. After World War I French troops took over the Ruhr Valley. They wanted to take coal as part of the fines Germany had to pay for starting the war. But today Germany is a pioneer in cleaner forms of energy. Many people have stopped using coal, and the mines are now less busy.

Germany also has a large chemical industry. The industry relies on its great rivers and natural resources. The biggest factories are built on rivers, so that raw materials can be brought in and finished products sent out on barges.

▲ The Rhine-Main-Danube Canal makes a huge bend through the Bavarian hills. The long canal connects the Rhine, Main, and Danube rivers and allows barges to sail from the North Sea to the Black Sea on the other side of Europe.

Humans and Nature

GERMANS TRADITIONALLY BELIEVE THAT storks bring good luck to people on whose houses they nest. In the country, people build platforms on their roofs for the birds' nests to make sure that the birds keep returning. White storks spend the winter in Africa, but fly home to Germany each spring. Storks build large nests. Rather than make the same effort every year, they often reuse an old nest to raise their chicks before the long trip back to Africa in the fall.

The close relationship between people and storks is mirrored in close links with other animals, which Germans have raised or hunted for centuries. Yet there are still areas of Germany where humans have had little impact on wildlife or the original vegetation.

◀ A white stork calls while guarding her newly hatched chick. Both parents work together to build the nest, which can be 6 feet (2 m) wide.

At a Glance

PROTECTED PARADISES

The map opposite shows vegetation zones—or what grows where—in Germany. Vegetation zones form ecosystems, environments that support specific plants and animals. Today there are 97 nature reserves in Germany. The biggest protected area is the Black Forest, where two reserves cover about 2,875 square miles (7,450 square km). One very beautiful national park is on Usedom, a sandy island in the Baltic Sea.

Species at Risk

Although the German government works hard to protect the country's wildlife, some species are still in danger of extinction. Species at risk include:

> Bank vole (mammal)
> Basking shark
> Bavarian freshwater snail
> Beluga whale
> Blue ground beetle
> Eurasian otter
> European beaver
> European mink
> Garden dormouse

> Geoffroy's bat
> Great raft spider
> Harbor porpoise
> Houbara bustard (bird)
> Ibex
> Minke whale
> Noble crayfish
> Northern right whale
> Pond bat
> Red-breasted goose

▼ The chamois, a wild relative of goats and sheep, lives in the mountains of southern Germany. The animal's skin makes very soft leather, which was traditionally used for cleaning and polishing.

SWEDEN

Baltic Sea

DENMARK

North Sea

SEALS ON A
SANDBANK,
page 20

North Frisian Islands

Schleswig-
Holstein
Wadden Sea
N.P.

Fehmarn

Vorpommern
Lagoon Area N.P.

Jasmund
N.P.

Rügen

● Kiel

● Rostock

HUNTERS WITH
WILD BOAR,
page 22

Hamburg
Wadden Sea N.P.

East Frisian Islands

Lower Saxony
Wadden Sea N.P.

Hamburg ●

Elbe

Müritz

Müritz N.P.

STORK,
pages 2, 16–17

Lower Oder
Valley N.P.

POLAND

NETHERLANDS

Ems

Weser

Aller

MITTELLAND CANAL

Hanover ●

Berlin ✪

Oder

Ruhr

Harz N.P.

H a r z

Saale

Elbe

Leipzig ●

Neisse

LYNX,
page 20

Düsseldorf ●

Köln
(Cologne) ●

Kellerwald-
Edersee N.P.

Hainich
N.P.

Saxon
Switzerland N.P.

Bonn ●

Hohnes
Venn-Eifel
N.P.

Rhine

BELGIUM

Mosel

Taunus

Frankfurt ●

Mainz ●

Main

R H U N E - M A N - D A N U B E   C A N A L

Ore Mountains

Bohemian Forest

CZECH
REPUBLIC

LUXEMBOURG

Neckar

Rhine

Black Forest

Stuttgart ●

Schwäbische Alb

Danube

Danube

Bavarian
Forest N.P.

BROWN BEAR,
page 21

FRANCE

ADDER,
page 23

München
(Munich) ●

Lake
Constance

Bavarian Alps

AUSTRIA

Berchtesgaden
N.P.

LIECHTENSTEIN

SWITZERLAND

ITALY

MAP KEY

**Primary vegetation
zones/ecosystems**

▢ Temperate broadleaf forest

▢ Temperate coniferous forest

Protected lands

▢ National park

Vegetation & Ecosystems Map

A Forested Land

Germany's major unspoiled habitats lie in two main regions. The flat northern coast is home to sea life and wading birds, while the forested hills and mountains farther south are the best places to see wildcats, boar, ibex, and other large mammals.

Before the first people settled and began to farm in the region about 6,000 years ago, the country was almost entirely covered in forest; the rest was marshland. As in most of northern Europe, nearly all of the ancient forests are gone. They were cleared from lowland areas to make way for farms, or trees died when farmers diverted water away from them to irrigate their fields.

▲ A Eurasian lynx—a relative of the bobcat—in a woodland reserve in eastern Germany

▼ Gray seals rest on a sandbank on Germany's North Sea coast.

GET BRUNO!

Brown bears were common in Germany until they became a favorite prey for hunters. By the middle of the 19th century, wild bears had disappeared.

At the start of the 21st century, the Italians reintroduced bears to the wild on their side of the Alps. But animals do not observe national borders. One bear crossed the mountains in May 2006. It was the first wild bear to be seen in Germany since 1835.

Villagers in the Bavarian Alps were excited by the newcomer, whom they named Bruno. But the bear became a nuisance, killing animals. Hunters used darts to drug Bruno and move him away from populated areas. The bear soon returned. He was so bold that people grew afraid that he might attack someone. The hunters returned, this time to kill Bruno.

▲ Apart from Bruno, brown bears are found only in German wildlife reserves and zoos.

However, today about one-third of Germany is still wooded, which is more land than in most similar European countries. These forests are different from the original woodland, however. They have been planted to provide timber and firewood.

Germany's ancient forests contained oak, hornbeam, and beech trees. Those species still grow, but are now also joined by foreign varieties, such as spruces and Japanese larch. Germany's location in central Europe means that it has colder winters than other countries farther west, such as France and Belgium. As a result, German forests contain many conifers, such as firs and pines, which thrive in cold conditions.

Hunting in the Trees

The forests and secluded hills of rural Germany are home to many animals and birds that are good to eat. There is a long tradition of hunting in Germany. The hunters' largest common targets are roe deer; chamois and ibex, two types of wild goat, live on the rocky slopes of the Alps. Hares are almost everywhere, and there are large numbers of quails and pheasants.

▲ At the end of a day's hunting, hunters blow on traditional horns. A different note is blown in honor of each animal killed—in this case, wild boar.

Animals are protected from hunting if their numbers drop. But the German authorities allow hunting again when populations rise. Wild boars were protected for much of the late 20th century, for example. When they began to damage crops, the law was changed so that they could be shot to keep their numbers down.

Wild Killers

There are some big hunters left in the wild, too. While there are almost no wolves left, apart from the odd stray that crosses the border from the Czech Republic, and no bears, there are many wildcats—the wild ancestors of pet cats—in the Harz mountains. The far

A MASKED INVADER

In the last 50 years, an Asian animal has made a home in Germany's forests. Raccoon dogs are originally from Siberia and Japan, but in the middle of the 20th century they were brought to Germany and other parts of Europe to be farmed for their fur. Some soon escaped and their numbers started to grow.

At first glance, the animals look like raccoons. They are about the same size and have the same striped tail and mask-like pattern over their eyes. But raccoons live only in the Americas, not in Asia or Europe. Raccoon dogs are actually related to foxes. They live in pairs or small families. They hunt for mice and scoop snails from rivers, but they can also survive on garbage.

▲ Raccoon dogs are thought to look and live a lot like early ancestors of foxes, wolves, and other types of dog.

east is home to lynxes, another kind of hunting cat. The central and southern hills are home to smaller carnivores, such as foxes, polecats, and badgers.

Birdlife

The lakes and wetlands along Germany's coastlines are important stopover points for many migrating birds. The German government has set up reserves for the birds' protection. There are also golden eagles in the Bavarian Alps, and sharp-eyed observers might spot a rare white-tailed eagle hunting over the northern plains.

▼ An adder prepares to bite in a meadow in Bavaria. Adders are the only poisonous snakes in Germany.

Divided No More

FOR NEARLY 30 YEARS, BERLIN, the capital of Germany, was divided by a wall that split the city. Armed guards patrolled the wall, and anyone who tried to cross without permission was shot dead. Germany had been split into two countries at the end of World War II (1939–1945). The barrier was built suddenly by the communist government of East Germany in 1961 to stop its citizens from seeking a better life in West Germany, which seemed more liberal and was far richer. The wall split neighbor from neighbor; families could not see their relatives face to face. In 1989, however, the communist system collapsed. The guards on the wall left their posts. Berliners rushed to party on top of the hated wall and to pull it down. The whole of Germany was reunified soon afterward.

◀ A crowd gathers at a gap in the Berlin Wall in November 1989 to celebrate the end of the border that had divided Berlin in two.

A HOLY EMPIRE

I n some ways, the division of Germany after World War II was not unusual. It has only been a united country for a relatively short time. Until the late 19th century, it was made up of many smaller states. The states did combine, however, to form larger groupings. The most powerful was the Holy Roman Empire, which in various forms lasted from 800 to 1806. It was created when the Pope in Rome crowned Charlemagne the emperor of an empire that stretched across western Europe.

At various times over the centuries, the Holy Roman Empire's shape echoed that of modern Germany. It fought to protect the Catholic Church after the birth of the Protestant faith in Germany in 1517, following the Reformation.

▲ The crown of the Holy Roman Empire was worn by most German emperors between the 11th and 18th centuries. It is kept in Vienna, Austria, and will only be returned to Germany if the country is ruled by a Holy Roman emperor once again.

The last Holy Roman emperor, Francis II, gave up the throne in 1806. The French leader Napoleon Bonaparte broke the empire up.

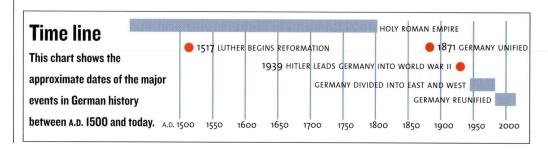

Time line

This chart shows the approximate dates of the major events in German history between A.D. 1500 and today.

HOLY ROMAN EMPIRE

1517 LUTHER BEGINS REFORMATION

1871 GERMANY UNIFIED

1939 HITLER LEADS GERMANY INTO WORLD WAR II

GERMANY DIVIDED INTO EAST AND WEST

GERMANY REUNIFIED

A.D. 1500   1550   1600   1650   1700   1750   1800   1850   1900   1950   2000

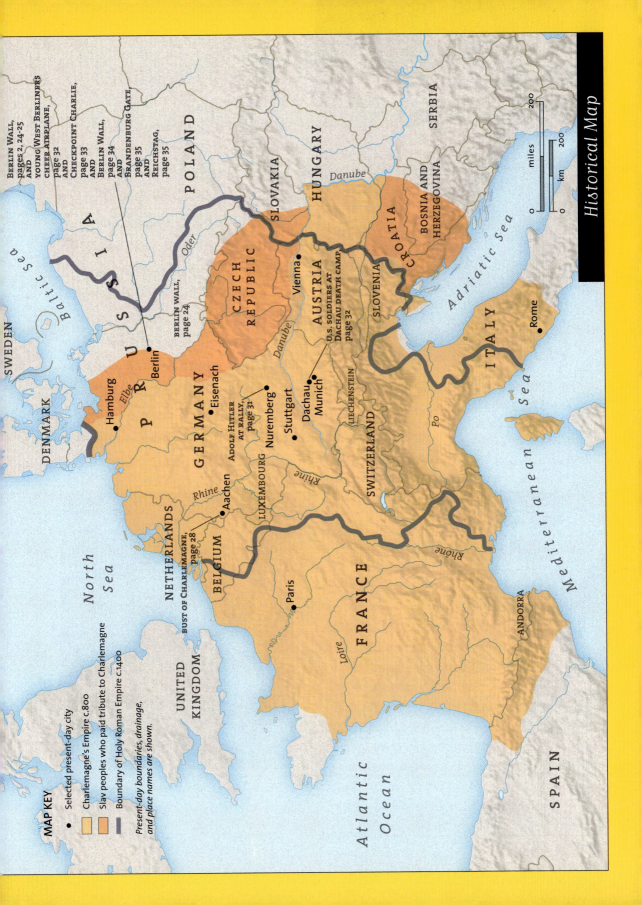

Historical Map

MAP KEY

- Selected present-day city
  - Charlemagne's Empire c.800
  - Slav peoples who paid tribute to Charlemagne
  - Boundary of Holy Roman Empire c.1400

Present-day boundaries, drainage, and place names are shown.

BERLIN WALL, page 24

BUST OF CHARLEMAGNE, page 28

ADOLF HITLER AT RALLY, page 31

U.S. SOLDIERS AT DACHAU DEATH CAMP, page 32

BERLIN WALL, pages 2, 24-25 AND YOUNG WEST BERLINERS CHEER AIRPLANE, page 32 AND CHECKPOINT CHARLIE, page 33 AND BERLIN WALL, page 34 AND BRANDENBURG GATE, page 35 AND REICHSTAG, page 35

SWEDEN

DENMARK

Baltic Sea

North Sea

UNITED KINGDOM

NETHERLANDS

BELGIUM

LUXEMBOURG

Atlantic Ocean

FRANCE

Paris

Loire

Rhine

Aachen

Rhine

Hamburg

Elbe

Berlin

P R U S S I A

GERMANY

Eisenach

Nuremberg

Stuttgart

Munich

Dachau

SWITZERLAND

LIECHTENSTEIN

Rhône

Po

ITALY

Rome

Mediterranean Sea

ANDORRA

SPAIN

POLAND

Oder

CZECH REPUBLIC

SLOVAKIA

Danube

AUSTRIA

Vienna

Danube

HUNGARY

SLOVENIA

CROATIA

BOSNIA AND HERZEGOVINA

SERBIA

Adriatic Sea

miles 0   200
km 0   200

A golden bust of Charlemagne at Aachen Cathedral, the capital from which he controlled much of Europe.

Coming Together

Humans began to settle in northern Europe about 10,000 years ago, after the end of the last Ice Age. The first people to speak a language similar to modern German probably lived in the area about 5,000 years ago. It was still thousands of years before Germany was created, however. Before 1871, it was a patchwork of small states ruled by dukes and kings. Many of the states were also part of the Holy Roman Empire but kept their distinct identities even though their citizens all spoke German and shared many traditions. There were often wars among the different states, particularly after the

MARTIN LUTHER

At the start of the 1500s, some Catholic priests in Germany sold people pardons for their sins. Many people were horrified that it might be possible to buy a place in heaven. They included a German monk named Martin Luther (1483–1546), who began to protest the corruption. His actions were among the main causes of the Reformation, which saw many Christians break away from the Catholic Church. They created new churches based on Luther's teachings, known as Protestantism. It aimed to weaken the power of the clergy in worship.

Martin Luther is shown surrounded by other religious reformers in a painting from the 1500s.

Reformation. The Reformation began a new branch of Christianity, splitting Germany—and the rest of Europe. Some German states became Protestant; others stayed part of the Catholic Church.

A change came in 1871. Otto von Bismarck, a politician from the powerful state of Prussia, used a combination of alliances and warfare to bring the other states together. The unified nation was ruled by the emperor Wilhelm I from Berlin.

Power Struggle

Late in the 19th century, Germany began competing with other European countries to set up colonies in Africa and Asia. Tension between the European powers eventually led to the outbreak of World War I (1914–1918). Germany and its allies were defeated by Britain, France, the United States, and their allies. It was the worst conflict the world had seen: millions of troops and civilians died.

The peace settlement took away Germany's territories abroad and gave parts of Germany itself to its neighbors. As a punishment for starting the war,

▲ German soldiers practice putting on gas masks during World War I. The masks protected troops against chemical weapons; even the soldiers' dogs had to wear them.

PLAYING WITH MONEY

After its defeat in World War I, Germany had to pay vast fines, called reparations, to the victors. It printed more banknotes to pay, but the result was that the value of the currency, the Deutsche Mark, fell steeply. People needed huge sums to buy even basics. By 1923, it took a wheelbarrow full of cash to buy a loaf of bread. The bills were worth so little that people used them to light fires. Children used thick wads of banknotes as building blocks.

▶ **A man uses worthless German banknotes to paper his wall in 1923.**

Germany was fined a huge sum to pay for rebuilding what had been destroyed in the conflict.

Nazi Germany

The German economy collapsed under the strain of paying the fines, and the government found it difficult to rebuild the country and restore order. Germans looked for a leader who could make Germany great again. Adolf Hitler led the tiny National Socialist Party, or NSDAP for short. He became popular by blaming other people—such as the Allies or Europe's Jews—for Germany's problems. In 1933, he used his

popularity to become German chancellor. Soon, he began to rule as a dictator. He expanded the army and navy and took back some territory that Germany had lost. In September 1939, however, when Hitler invaded Poland, the other large European countries decided to stop him. World War II had begun.

At first, the German forces were unstoppable. By 1940, Hitler governed much of central and eastern Europe. In 1941 Hitler sent troops into the vast Soviet Union—the name for Russia's huge communist empire. The Germans reached the outskirts of Moscow, but the army was stretched too thin. The Russians began

▲ Adolf Hitler salutes young Nazis at a rally in Nuremberg before World War II. Hitler believed that the Germans were a master race who would rule the world for a thousand years. He called this race Aryans.

to push the Germans back. The Germans were being beaten by the British on other fronts, too. The United States joined the war on the Allied side. The tide had turned. By 1944, the Germans were under attack from three sides. As the Russians entered Berlin in April 1945, Hitler killed himself.

Allied troops advancing into Germany found evidence of what would come to be called the Holocaust. The Nazis had built death camps to kill Europe's Jews and other excluded groups, such as the Roma (gypsies). The camps had chambers where dozens of people could be killed at once with poisonous gas. Up to nine million people died in the camps.

▲ U.S. soldiers examine a gas chamber at the concentration camp in Dachau, Bavaria, in 1945.

The Great Divide

After the war, Germany was divided into four zones, controlled by the major Allies. Three regions were soon reunited as West Germany, but the Soviet-

▼ Children in West Berlin wave at a plane bringing food during the Berlin Airlift.

controlled East Germany was separate. The border
between the two became part of the boundary
between the world's new enemies: the capitalist West
and the communist East, led by the Soviet Union. This
boundary was often called the "Iron Curtain."

The confrontation between East and West was
known as the Cold War, and the city of Berlin was its
center. Although it lay in East Germany, as the capital
Berlin was also split into four zones. There were
British, French, and American zones in West Berlin.
The Soviets controlled East Berlin. In 1948, the Soviets
attempted to force the other powers out of Berlin by
stopping supplies from passing through East Germany.
The West responded by flying in food and fuel. The
operation became known as the Berlin Airlift. It lasted
almost a year, and planes flew night and day, bringing

▲ Checkpoint Charlie
was the main crossing
point between East and
West Berlin during the
Cold War.

▲ East German guards stand on the Berlin Wall as a crowd of West Berliners gather on November 9, 1989, to demand that it be torn down.

millions of tons of supplies to the West Berliners, who were completely encircled by East Germany.

However, that was just the beginning in a long struggle for control of Berlin. By 1961, more than two million people had already fled from East to West. The East German government built a wall around West Berlin to stop its citizens from escaping.

Together at Last

The Soviet Union controlled East Germany for the next 30 years. In the 1970s, however, the economy of the Eastern Bloc—Russia, East Germany, and the other countries of Eastern Europe—grew weaker. In the 1980s, Soviet leader Mikhail Gorbachev began a program to make his government more liberal. In turn,

THE GATEWAY TO GERMANY

The Brandenburg Gate is one of the most famous structures in Germany and has been a powerful symbol of the country throughout its history. The top of the gate has a statue of the goddess of victory in a chariot. The Nazis used that as a symbol of the might of their new Germany. In 1961, the gate was the first place to be divided by the Berlin Wall. U.S. president John F. Kennedy came to the gate in 1963 and famously said, "Ich bin ein Berliner!" ("I am a Berliner!") Kennedy meant that he (and all Americans) were citizens of Berlin and would support West Germany against the communist Eastern Bloc. However, there was a little confusion at first because in German the word "berliner" also means "doughnut!"

▲ The Brandenburg Gate was completed in 1793. It is the main gate to the historic city of Berlin—and the only gate left standing. The gate is now fully restored to its former glory.

Eastern Europeans demanded more freedom. Some border controls were relaxed. Thousands of people poured through the "Iron Curtain" into the West.

On November 9, 1989, East Germany opened its borders. That night, joyful crowds used hammers and picks to knock the wall down. The East German government collapsed days later, and in October 1990, Germany again became a single nation. It was a triumphant moment, but it also began a series of new problems for the country. Merging the run-down economy of East Germany with modern West Germany would prove a challenging task.

▼ A German flag flies above a crowd celebrating Germany's reunification in 1990 outside the Reichstag—Germany's parliament building in Berlin.

A Mix
of
People

I N THE 2000 EUROPEAN CUP SOCCER FINALS,
Mehmet Scholl played for the German national
team. He was the first player of Turkish descent to
do so. For many Germans, Scholl's success was the
first time they had celebrated the country's
changing makeup. Today, almost one in every ten
Germans comes from a foreign country. That is more
than at any time in history. The largest minority are
Turks, who make up about 2.5 percent of the
population. They started coming in the 1950s to work,
and many stayed. Germany also has many people who
have come to escape violence in countries such as Sri
Lanka, Bosnia, and Vietnam. Even Jews are moving
back, mainly from Poland and Russia. Germany has
come a long way from the racist attitudes of the Nazis.

◀ **Mehmet Scholl (center) plays for the German national soccer team during the
European Cup in 2000. He was the first person with a Turkish parent to play on
the national team.**

COUNTRYWIDE CHANGES

T he official German language is called *Hochdeutsch*—High German, but there are many other dialects spoken across the country. Low German is the dialect spoken close to the sea in the north of the country. Bavarian is the main dialect in the south.

More German people die than are born each year. As result, the German population is going down, and the average age of a German is getting older. By 2050, a third of all Germans will be over 65, and the population will be lower than it was in 1950.

► Performers in the town of Herbstein celebrate the work of the Brothers Grimm. The brothers are among the most popular of all German writers. They made many traditional German fairy stories world famous.

Common German Phrases

G ermans call their language Deutsch, not German. Here are a few German words and phrases you might hear in Germany:

Guten Tag (GOO-ten taag)	Hello
Ja (yah)	Yes
Nein (nine)	No
Bitte (bit-TER)	Please
Danke (dan-KER)	Thank you
Ich heisse... (ikh HIGH–ser)	My name is...
Wie geht's? (vee GATES)	How are you?
Sprechen Sie Englisch? (sprek-un zee IN-glish?)	Do you speak English?
Wie bitte? (vee bit-TER?)	Pardon?
Auf Wiedersehen (owf VEE-der-say-en)	Goodbye

1950 / 68.4 million	1970 / 79.8 million	1990 / 82.2 million	2005 / 68.7 million
28% rural / 72% urban	20% rural / 80% urban	15% rural / 85% urban	12% rural / 88% urban

DENMARK

Baltic Sea

North Sea

Kiel

Rostock

Lübeck

Bremerhaven

Hamburg

HAMBURG TOWN HALL,
page 40

Oldenburg

Bremen

POLAND

BAUHAUS ARCHIVE,
page 44

Berlin

Wolfsburg

Potsdam

Hanover

NETHERLANDS

Osnabrück

Brunswick

Magdeburg

Cottbus

Bielefeld

Münster

Goslar

CHRISTMAS MARKET,
page 47

Hamm

Paderborn

Göttingen

Halle

Leipzig

Gelsenkirchen

Essen

Dortmund

Duisburg

Bochum

CHEMISTRY
CLASS,
page 42

Kassel

Dresden

Krefeld

Wuppertal

Mönchen-
gladbach

Düsseldorf

Leverkusen

BREADMAKING,
page 45

Erfurt

Gera

Freiberg

Aachen

Cologne

STATUE OF
BEETHOVEN,
page 43

Alsfeld

Chemnitz

BELGIUM

Bonn

TRADITIONAL
HOUSES,
page 40

EAU DE COLOGNE BOTTLE,
page 41
AND
COLOGNE CATHEDRAL,
page 46

Koblenz

PARADE,
page 38

LUXEMBOURG

Weisbaden

Frankfurt

CZECH
REPUBLIC

Mainz

Offenbach

Darmstadt

Würzburg

Ludwigshafen

Mannheim

Heidelberg

Nuremberg

Regensburg

Saarbrücken

Heilbronn

FRANCE

Karlsruhe

Pforzheim

Stuttgart

Ingolstadt

Ulm

Augsburg

Freising

Freiburg

AUSTRIA

Munich

MAP KEY

People per
square mile

2500 and over

250–2449

125–249

26–112

2.5–24.9

Under 2.5

People per
square kilometer

Over 1000

100–999

50–99

10–49

1–9

Under 1

LIECHTESTEIN

Population of urban area

■ 1 million and over

▲ 500,000 to 1 million

● 250,000 to 500,000

• 100,000 to 250,000

ITALY

SLOVENIA

Population Map

▲ German cities combine the old and the new. Here a hydrogen-powered bus drives past Hamburg's town hall.

▼ Traditional houses in Erfurt, a historic town in eastern Germany

Family Life

Germany has one of the most modern economies in the world, and for most Germans life is much the same as in other industrialized countries. In rural areas, however, several generations of a family may still live together. Young people in the countryside are sometimes unable to afford homes of their own. In cities, on the other hand, children usually leave home when they get a job.

Most German families have only one or two children, and the

population is falling. That will have a big impact in the future. Fewer workers will have to support larger numbers of retired seniors.

In most families, both parents work. Often they have no choice. In the 1990s, wages gradually fell. Some couples need two incomes, particularly if they want to enjoy the kind of comfortable lifestyle that is common in Germany—but expensive.

Love and Marriage

About half of German couples who want to live together get married. In Germany, weddings may have two parts. First, there is a civil ceremony at a government office. Usually the next day, the couple

THE SMELL OF SUCCESS

One of the world's most famous men's perfumes comes from Germany—but it was invented by an Italian. Giovanni Maria Farina made the scent in 1709 in Cologne. He claimed that it captured "the smell of an Italian spring morning after the rain." He made sure that no one found out the exact ingredients of his potion, which he called Eau de Cologne ("Water of Cologne" in French). The potion was so successful that eventually all scents became known as colognes. The original is still widely regarded as the best, however. It is now known as 4711, after the street number of an early address where the cologne was made—and its formula is still a secret.

▲ A giant bottle of Eau de Cologne on display in the window of Glockengasse 4711, the perfumery where the famous fragrance was first mixed.

has a church service. Between the two ceremonies, some couples hold a *polterabend*, German for "rumble night." The event has its roots in folklore. The newlyweds and their friends noisily smash glass and pottery to frighten away the Devil.

An increasing number of young Germans live together without marrying. Today, nearly half of German couples under 35 are not married.

School System

School in Germany ends at lunchtime. That might sound as if being a student is easy, but that is not the case. School starts very early in the morning—at 7:30 A.M.—and students get many assignments to do at home.

Everyone has to go to school from the ages of 6 to 15. Elementary students all study the same subjects. After that, children go to one of three different types of school. More academic students attend a *gymnasium* (pronounced with a hard "g") until age 18. Students who study at *realschule* go to school until age 15, when they may train for a job in industry. Other

THE DEAF COMPOSER

▲ A statue of Beethoven in the town square of Bonn, the city of his birth in western Germany.

Even as a child, Ludwig van Beethoven (1770–1827) was recognized as a musical genius. At age 17 he was sent from his home city of Bonn to Austria so that the composer Wolfgang Amadeus Mozart could hear him play. Mozart was impressed.

Over the next ten years, Beethoven wrote two symphonies and many other pieces. But then, Beethoven began to go deaf. Within a few years he could hear nothing. Remarkably he went on to write much more, including seven more symphonies. They are among the most famous pieces of music ever written. Many people believe that they expressed the feelings that the composer could no longer express by chatting with other people. The deaf composer also continued conducting. At the end of one performance, Beethoven had to be turned around to face the audience so that he could see that they were clapping.

Beethoven was an odd man in many ways. He washed himself regularly, but insisted on wearing the dirtiest and scruffiest clothes imaginable. At the height of his fame, he was arrested in Vienna by a policeman who mistook him for a tramp.

students go to *hauptschule* (high school), where the pace is slower than at the other two schools.

Since the 1960s there has also been a fourth type of German school, the *gesamtschule*. It teaches students of all abilities in different classes. Some Germans think that such a system is fairer, because everyone goes to the same school. It also gives students more time to decide on what they want to do in life.

Keeping the Country Healthy

Germans traditionally have a good health-care system. The service is available to all, no matter how much money people have. But such a system does not come cheap for the society as a whole. All workers pay toward health insurance, and medical services are among the most expensive in the world. Recent cuts in funding have damaged the quality of the service.

Fine Arts

Germany has been called the "Land of Poets and Thinkers." It could just as easily be called the "Land of Composers and Artists." Germans are famous in all forms of art. Many important classical composers came from

▲ The Bauhaus Archive and Museum in Berlin. Bauhuas is a style of architecture and design that was developed in Germany in the 1920s.

Germany, for example: they include Johann Sebastian Bach, Johannes Brahms, Robert Schumann, and Richard Wagner. In the 18th century, Bach helped develop musical forms such as the concerto.

A century later another German, Ludwig van Beethoven, was the most important composer of a new kind of classical music. Its power and drama

echoed an artistic movement known as romanticism. The movement celebrated people's emotions. Its creators included the German writers Johann Wolfgang von Goethe and Friedrich von Schiller.

Famous German painters include Albrecht Dürer and Max Ernst. Ernst painted real objects in impossible arrangements, a style called surrealism. In the 1920s, the Bauhaus school changed the face of modern architecture. Its buildings had clean straight and curved lines and plain windows. They looked a little like factories, because the architects wanted to emphasize that buildings had a practical use.

Among more recent writers, novelist Günter Grass is one of the most celebrated. He won the 1999 Nobel Prize for Literature. He caused a scandal in 2006 when he admitted to having belonged to the Waffen-SS, a notorious Nazi armed unit. Grass is very popular in Germany, so his confession sparked a heated debate about how much people are to blame for their actions during World War II.

Hearty Food

German food varies from region to region, but many meals include meat and potatoes. The potatoes

NATIONAL HOLIDAYS

Most German holidays are based on the Christian calendar. One that is not is Unity Day, which marks the reunification of Germany in 1990.

JANUARY 1	New Year
JANUARY 6	Epiphany
SPRING	Good Friday/Easter Monday
MAY 1	Labor Day
MAY 24	Ascension Day
OCTOBER 3	Unity Day
DECEMBER 25–26	Christmas

▼ An elderly German sprinkles loaves of bread with salt before baking. Her husband will take the loaves to a bakehouse in the village for cooking.

are boiled or fried or made into dumplings. There may also be local vegetables, such as asparagus in spring or green cabbage in the fall. Specialty dishes include sausages. There are said to be up to 1,500 different sorts of sausage in Germany. They inspired the hot dogs and wieners enjoyed in North America. German desserts include cakes such as Black Forest torte (a rich chocolate cake with cherries and cream).

Germany is also famous for beer and wine. Its 1,200 breweries include the oldest in the world. The Weihenstephan brewery in Freising, Bavaria, started making beer in 1040. It was set up by monks, who sold the beer to raise money—but they also kept some for themselves.

▲ Most of Germany's vineyards are in the west of the country.

▼ Cologne Cathedral on the Rhine River dates from 1248.

Different Faiths

About two-thirds of Germans are Christians. There are nearly equal numbers of Protestants and Roman Catholics in the country. Most Protestants still live in the north and east, while most southern Germans are Catholic. The division dates from the Reformation in the 16th century.

More than one-quarter of Germans say that they have no religion. Of the rest, most are

OLD-STYLE CHRISTMAS

From the last week of November until Christmas Eve, the streets of German cities are transformed into markets that have a long history. The earliest began nearly 300 years ago so that craftspeople could sell their goods. Today, the wooden stalls still sell traditional handmade toys, candles, decorations, and nativity figures. The markets stay open after dark, when they twinkle with lights. The air fills with the smell of Christmas goodies: mulled or heated wine, roasted chestnuts, and grilled sausage. Food stands are everywhere: tired shoppers can enjoy traditional food or buy *lebkuchen*, spicy gingerbread cookies, to take home.

▲ At dusk, the Christmas market at Goslar in central Germany is bathed in twinkling lights.

Muslims, mainly of Turkish descent. The number of German Muslims is increasing. Within 20 years, a third of all German children will be Muslims.

A Sporty Nation

One in every three Germans belongs to a sports club, and 12 million others exercise regularly. The most popular sport is soccer, which is played by 6 million Germans and watched by millions more on TV. The other main sports are tennis and shooting—both at targets and hunting animals. Popular team sports are handball, volleyball, and basketball.

Triumph
from
Defeat

ANGELA MERKEL'S ELECTION as German chancellor in 2005 was a narrow victory. The first female chancellor, Merkel was also the first from the former East Germany. Her election victory was symbolic. It was a sign that, at least in some ways, the differences between West and East Germany are fading away.

In 1945, Germany was in ruins and divided into West and East. With aid from the West, West Germany recovered to become Europe's richest country. East Germany, under communist control, fell far behind.

The Germans always hoped to reunite their country. The chance came with the collapse of communism in 1989. The reunited nation has made many advances, as symbolized by Merkel's election.

◀ A portrait of Angela Merkel is added to those of all the chancellors since 1949. Merkel was elected at the age of 51, the youngest leader of modern Germany.

SHARING POWER

Germany is a federal republic made up of 16 states, or *länder*. The capital, Berlin, is both a city and a federal state; so, too, are Bremen and Hamburg. The other 13 *länder* have their own capitals. Many are large cities, such as Stuttgart in Baden-Württemberg and Munich in Bavaria. Other capitals are smaller towns that have always been their regions' traditional centers.

A *länd* (singular form of *länder*) is governed by an assembly of elected lawmakers. Länder are split into *kreise*, or counties. These are divided into *gemeinden*, or parishes.

Trading Partners

Germany's main trading partner is France. The next most important is the United States, followed by other nations of the European Union (EU). Germany is now the world's biggest exporter, having overtaken the United States in 2003. Its most profitable foreign sales come from automobiles and chemicals.

Country	Percent Germany exports
France	10.2%
United States	8.8%
United Kingdom	7.9%
All others combined	73.1%

Country	Percent Germany imports
France	8.7%
Netherlands	8.5%
United States	6.6%
All others combined	75.7%

▼ Inside the dome of the Reichstag in Berlin (also shown on page 1), the public can look down into the chamber where laws are made.

Political Map

Learning from the Past

After the war, Germans were determined not to repeat the mistakes of the 1930s, when they elected an extreme politician who then set up a dictatorship. To avoid a repeat of the Nazi rise to power, West Germany drew up a new constitution in 1949. This *Grundgesetz* (Basic Law) guaranteed everyone basic rights. All Germans could own property, travel freely, join trade unions, and be equal under the law.

At the time, East Germans could not benefit from the *Grundgesetz*. All the same, the lawyers who drafted the law prepared for the possibility that they might at some point in the future.

HOW THE GOVERNMENT WORKS

Germany is a federal republic. The president is the head of state, but the role is ceremonial. Power lies with the chancellor, who leads the government with the ministers of the cabinet. He or she is chosen by the parliament, which is divided into two chambers. One is the Bundestag (Federal Assembly), for which elections are held every four years. The other chamber is the Bundesrat (Federal Council). Its members are appointed by the governments of the länder and are chosen to reflect the public support for various political parties. Federal judges are all elected by members of the Bundestag and Bundesrat. The federal courts oversee the work of the länder courts.

PRESIDENT		
EXECUTIVE (PRESIDENT)	LEGISLATIVE (PARLIAMENT)	JUDICIARY
CHANCELLOR	BUNDESRAT 69 MEMBERS	FEDERAL COURTS
CABINET	BUNDESTAG 600 MEMBERS	LÄNDER COURTS

Tale of Two Nations

The West German government always intended to reunite the country. The goal remained impossible as long as East Germany was controlled by the Soviet Union. The government in Moscow was determined to keep Germany divided. They reasoned that a divided Germany could never again attack the Soviet Union as it had done under Hitler. More than 20 million Russians had been killed by Hitler's army.

Meanwhile, the West German government was based in Bonn, on the Rhine River. The government concentrated on making the nation prosperous, with spectacular results. With aid provided under the European Recovery Program, West Germany rebuilt its industries. In 1957 the nation joined its old enemies— including France, Belgium, and the Netherlands—to form a trading region known as the Common Market. Members of the Common Market later formed the European Union (EU), a joint body to oversee trade, foreign relations, and lawmaking. At the start of 2007, the EU had 27 member nations.

Painful Reunion

When the communist regime of East Germany collapsed in 1989, West Germany kept its long-standing

▲ The West German Bundestag in session in Bonn in the 1970s.

▼ The European Central Bank (ECB) is located in Frankfurt, the financial center of Germany. The ECB manages the euro (€), the EU's currency.

INDUSTRY

This map shows Germany's main centers of industry, mining, and manufacturing. Germany is one of the most heavily industrialized nations on Earth.

MAP KEY

- Manufacturing center
- Steel manufacturing
- Processing plant
- Coal mining
- ▲ Kaolin
- ◆ Potash
- ○ Salt

promise to welcome back its neighbor. That was easier said than done: the East had slipped so far economically that even the wealth of West Germany was barely enough to solve its problems. Factories were inefficient; some were so old that they were not safe for workers and had to be closed. Although the West had always promised to exchange East German Ostmarks one-for-one with West German Deutsche Marks, on the morning of Unity Day—October 3, 1990—it was not possible. The former was worthless, while the latter was the world's strongest currency.

Since reunification the German economy has slowed down. The government has to spend about $70 billion a year to modernize the East. Much of the money goes to create work for millions of East Germans, or in slang, *Ossis*. (West Germans are the *Wessis*.) Although Germany is poorer than West Germany was before, it is still the world's fifth-largest economy.

Manufacturing Money

Germany makes most of its money from manufacturing. In the east, industrial areas are close to the Elbe and

THE CAR OF THE PEOPLE

When Adolf Hitler came to power in 1933, he promised that every German family would own an automobile. He contacted the Austrian engineer Ferdinand Porsche, who later founded the famous sports car firm that bears his name. Hitler ordered Porsche to design a car that would carry two adults and three children and cost no more than 6 months' average wages. Two years later, Porsche unveiled the KdF-Wagen—the initials stood for Kraft durch Freude ("Strength through Joy"). The first models were built at the Daimler-Benz factory in Stuttgart.

The car was an immediate hit. Its resounding success began after World War II, when it became known as the Beetle—mainly

▲ Beetles may not be the fastest or most comfortable cars—but they can be a lot of fun!

because of its rounded shape. Beginning in 1945 the car was produced by Volkswagen (VW), which means "people's car". By 2003, more than 21 million had been built. That made it the best-selling car in history—and it's still going.

Saale rivers around the cities of Leipzig, Dresden, and Chemnitz. In the west, coal and steel are produced in the Ruhr region around Essen and Dortmund. The chemical industry is located farther south along the Rhine. The centers of automobile manufacturing are in Munich, Stuttgart, and Wolfsburg.

The fame of Germany's biggest companies— Adidas, Volkswagen, Siemens, BASF, and Bayer—hides another major strength of the nation's economy: the high number of small companies. Some 98 percent of German companies have fewer than 500 employees,

THERE'S NO LIMIT

I n most countries even the fastest roads have speed limits. In Germany the freeways—known as autobahnen—have fewer restrictions than anywhere else in the developed world. Drivers have to slow down in bad weather, on winding stretches of road, and in long tunnels, but on about 40 percent of the network, drivers can go as fast as they like.

Not many cars comfortably go over about 90 miles per hour (144 km/h), but several German models can. The Porsche 911 has a top speed of 182 miles per hour (293 km/h), and the BMW M3 Coupe is fitted with a limiter that restricts its top speed to 155 miles per hour (249 km/h).

Well-designed cars make driving safer. Despite the high speeds, the chance of being killed in a car accident in Germany is half that of the risk in the United States.

▲ Germany's freeways (autobahnen) were the earliest in the world. The first was opened near Berlin in 1921.

and 80 percent of Germans work for one of them. Most small companies are owned by and employ middle-class people. A successful middle class is key to modern Germany's stability and success.

Sights to See

Germany is an increasingly popular vacation destination for Europeans, particularly with people who want to visit wilderness areas away from crowds. The North Sea coast can be chilly, but is excellent for

sailing and surfing. Inland there are 350 spa towns, where visitors bathe in water from underground springs. Since Roman times, people have believed that minerals in the water make it beneficial for their health. The best known spa is at Baden-Baden in the Black Forest.

Bavaria is particularly rich in attractions, such as Neuschwanstein, a fairy-tale castle built in the 19th century by "Mad" King Ludwig II. In late September the state capital, Munich, hosts Oktoberfest, a two-week festival that attracts six million visitors each year.

After the first snowfall, the Alps are a popular destination for skiers. Many Germans are concerned about the effect of such tourism on the environment. Such issues are increasingly addressed on an international level. Germany will need to work with its neighbors and the EU in order to best safeguard its natural treasures.

▲ **Neuschwanstein Castle in Bavaria is one of Germany's most photographed buildings.**

▼ **Kaiser Wilhelm Church, one of the many sights of Berlin, was left in ruins after World War II as a reminder of Germany's violent past.**

Add a Little Extra to Your Country Report!

I f you are assigned to write a report about Germany, you'll want to include basic information about the country, of course. The Fast Facts chart on page 8 will give you a good start. The rest of the book will give you the details you need to create a full and up-to-date paper or PowerPoint presentation. But what can you do to make your report more fun than anyone else's? If you use your imagination and dig a bit deeper into some of the topics introduced in this book, you're sure to come up with information that will make your report unique!

>Flag

Perhaps you could explain the history of Germany's flag, and the meanings of its colors. Go to **www.crwflags .com/fotw/flags** for more information.

>National Anthem

How about downloading Germany's national anthem and playing it for your class? At **www.nationalanthems.info** you'll find what you need, including the words to the anthem, plus sheet music. Simply pick "G" and then "Germany" from the list on the left-hand side of the screen, and you're on your way.

>Time Difference

If you want to understand the time difference between Germany and where you are, this Web site can help: **www.worldtimeserver.com**. Just pick "Germany" from the list on the left. If you called Germany right now, would you wake whomever you are calling from their sleep?

>Currency

Another Web site will convert your money into euros, the currency used in Germany. You'll want to know how much money to bring if you're ever lucky enough to travel to Germany: **www.xe.com/ucc**.

>Weather

Why not check the current weather in Germany? It's easy—simply go to **www.weather.com** to find out if it's sunny or cloudy, warm or cold in Germany right this minute! Pick "World" from the headings at the top of the page. Then search for Germany. Click on any city you like. Be sure to click on the tabs below the weather report for Sunrise/Sunset information, Weather Watch, and Business Travel Outlook, too. Scroll down the page for the 36-hour forecast and a satellite weather map. Compare your weather to the weather in the German city you chose. Is this a good season, weather-wise, for a person to travel to Germany?

>Miscellaneous

Still want more information? Simply go to National Geographic's One-Stop Research site at **www.nationalgeographic.com/onestop**. It will help you find maps, photos and art, articles and information, games, and features that you can use to jazz up your report.

Glossary

Architecture the art of desiging buildings.

Causeway a long bridge that crosses the sea to connect an island to the mainland. Some causeways are covered by water at high tide.

Chancellor the head of government in some countries, including Germany.

Circa a Latin word meaning "about": it is sometimes abbreviated to "ca."

Concentration camp a detention center where prisoners are gathered together. The Nazis used concentration camps to exterminate Jews and others during the Holocaust.

Communism a system of government where a single political party rules a country with the job of ensuring that wealth is shared equally among all the people in the country. East Germany was a communist country between 1945 and 1990.

Dialect a regional variation of a language with some words, spellings, and pronunciations that differ from the standard form of the language.

Dictator a leader who has complete control over a country and does not have to be elected or reelected to office regularly. There are no government controls to keep a dictator from becoming cruel and corrupt.

Ethnic group a large group of people who share a common ancestry or background.

Generation the members of a family that are all about the same age—brothers and sisters and their cousins. Their parents are an older generation, while their children are the younger generation.

Holocaust the murder of millions of Jews, Roma (Gypsies), homosexuals, disabled people, and political enemies in Nazi Germany's death camps.

Ice Age a period when the Earth was colder than it is now and ice covered continents in the north and south.

Legislation making laws.

Middle Ages the period of history between the 5th and 15th centuries.

Migration the annual movement of animals, such as birds, deer, or whales, from one place to another.

Protestant a Christian who belongs to one of several churches that broke away from the Catholic Church in the 16th century.

Reformation a split in the Christian church in western Europe in the 16th century.

Reunification when separated groups are brought back together to make a whole again.

Roman Catholic a Christian who follows the branch of the religion based in Rome, Italy.

Soviet Union a large empire of communist states that existed between 1917 and 1990. The union included countries such as Russia, Ukraine, and Armenia, which are now independent from one other.

Species a type of organism; animals or plants in the same species look similar and can only breed successfully among themselves.

Toll a charge when a vehicle travels along a stretch of road or river, or over a bridge.

Wilderness a region that is generally undisturbed by human beings.

Bibliography

Kappler, Arno. *Facts about Germany*. Frankfurt/Main: Societätsverlag, 2000.

Walker, Ida. *Germany*. Philadelphia: Mason Crest Publishers, 2006.

http://www.bundesregierung
.de/Webs/Breg/EN/Homepage
/home.html
(government Web site)

http://www.rootsweb.com/
~deubadnw/history/maps/
maps.htm
(historical maps of Germany)

http://www.tatsachen-ueber-
deutschland.de/en/
(general information)

Further Information

NATIONAL GEOGRAPHIC Articles

Curry, Andrew. "Berlin, Germany." NATIONAL GEOGRAPHIC TRAVELER (September 2006): 119.

McKelway, Margaret. "The Case Of The King Who Was Crazy for Castles." NATIONAL GEOGRAPHIC KIDS (August 1996): 3.

Web sites to explore

More fast facts about Germany, from the CIA (Central Intelligence Agency): https://www.cia.gov/cia/publications/factbook/geos/gm.html

How did Martin Luther change Germany and the world? Find out about the man who split the Roman Catholic Church with this biography produced by PBS:

http://www.pbs.org/empires/martinluther/about_driv.html

The Berlin Wall was a symbol of the division between the East and West. This feature from the BBC tells you about the day the Berlin Wall came into being:
http://news.bbc.co.uk/onthisday/hi/dates/stories/august/13/newsid_3054000/3054060.stm

Thinking about going to Germany one day? The government tourism site has all the information you will need: http://www.germany-tourism.de/

See, Hear

There are many ways to get a taste of life in Germany, including movies, TV shows, and magazines. You might be able to locate these:

Heimat
A long movie originally made as a TV series, *Heimat* ("Homeland") follows the same German family through a number of generations from the early 20th century until the 1980s.

The Atlantic Times
A newspaper produced in the United States to promote ties with Germany.

Wings of Desire
A movie made by Win Wenders about Berlin in the 1980s.

Run Lola, Run
A movie from 1999 that shows the creative energy of Germany after reunification.

Index

Credits

Picture Credits

Front Cover – Spine: Dainis Derics/Shutterstock; Top: Sissie Brimberg/NGIC; Low far left: Norbert Rosing/NGIC; Low left: Bernhaut/dpa/Corbis; Low right: Carsten Peter/NGIC; Low far right: Armin Weigel/dpa/Corbis.

Interior – Corbis: 31 up, 32 up; Atlantide Photo Travel: 13 up, 44 center; James L. Amos: 28 lo, 40 lo; Austrian Archives: 26 up; Bettmann: 29 up, 32 lo; Bojan Breceli/Sygma: 50 lo; Jens Buettner/epa: 3 right, 48-49; Regis Bossu/Sygma: 2-3, 24-25; Car Culture: 56 up; Jose Fuste Raga: 35 up; Todd Gipstein: 55 up; Paul Hardy: 14 lo, 57 lo; Roland Holschneider/dpa: 35 lo; Hulton-Deutsch Collection: 30 up; Pat Jerroldi/Papilio: 18 lo; Wolfgang Kaehler: 41 lo; Steve Kaufman: 23 lo; Walter Maeyers Edwards: 28 up; Michael Nicholson: 43 up; Klaus Rose/dpa: 42 center; Santos/zefa: 5 up; Stefan Sauer/dpa: 22 up; Bernd Settnik/dpa: TP; Sygma: 3 left, 36-37; Peter Turnley: 34 up; Nik Wheeler: 11 lo; NG Image Collection: Sisse Brimberg: 10 up, 47 up; Bruce Dale: 53 up; Taylor S. Kennedy: 12 up, 53 lo, 59 up; Sarah Leen: 40 up; Gerd Ludwig: 15 up, 38 lo, 45 lo, 46 lo, 57 up; George F. Mobley: 2 left, 6-7; Carsten Peter: 23 up; Steve Raymer: 33 up; Norbert Rosing: 2 right, 11 up, 16-17, 20 up, 20 lo, 21 up; Priit Vesilind: 13 lo;

For more information, please call 1-800-NGS-LINE (647-5463) or write to the following address:

NATIONAL GEOGRAPHIC SOCIETY
1145 17th Street N.W.
Washington, D.C. 20036-4688 U.S.A.

Visit the Society's Web site at www.nationalgeographic.com

Library of Congress Cataloging-in-Publication Data available on request
ISBN: 978-1-4263-0059-2

Printed in Belgium

Series design by Jim Hiscott.
The body text is set in Avenir; Knockout.
The display text is set in Matrix Script.

Front Cover—Top: Christmas market in Golsar; Low Far Left: Wildcat family; Low Left: Statue of Ludwig von Beethoven; Low Right: Enz Castle; Low Far Right: Workers in the BMW factory at Dingolfing

Page 1—The Reichstag in Berlin; Icon image on spine, Contents page, and throughout: Sans Souci Palace, Potsdam

Produced through the worldwide resources of the National Geographic Society

John M. Fahey, Jr., *President and Chief Executive Officer*; Gilbert M. Grosvenor, *Chairman of the Board*; Nina D. Hoffman, *Executive Vice President, President of Book Publishing Group*

National Geographic Staff for this Book

Nancy Laties Feresten, *Vice President, Editor-in-Chief of Children's Books*
Bea Jackson, *Director of Design and Illustration*
David M. Seager, *Art Director*
Virginia Koeth, *Project Editor*
Lori Epstein, *Illustrations Editor*
Stacy Gold, Nadia Hughes, *Illustrations Research Editors*
Mapping Specialists, *Maps*
Priyanka Lamichhane, *Assistant Editor*
R. Gary Colbert, *Production Director*
Lewis R. Bassford, *Production Manager*
Maryclare Tracy, Nicole Elliott *Manufacturing Managers*

Brown Reference Group plc. Staff for this Book

Volume Editor: Tom Jackson
Designer: Dave Allen
Picture Manager: Becky Cox
Maps: Martin Darlinson
Artwork: Darren Awuah
Index: Kay Ollerenshaw
Senior Managing Editor: Tim Cooke
Design Manager: Sarah Williams
Children's Publisher: Anne O'Daly
Editorial Director: Lindsey Lowe

About the Author

HENRY RUSSELL is a British author and broadcaster. After graduating from Oxford University, he traveled extensively, studying the business and social cultures of major European nations. He writes extensively for magazines, periodicals, and encyclopedias. This is his 14th book.

About the Consultants

DR. BENEDICT KORF is an assistant professor of human geography at the University of Zurich, Switzerland. His research focuses on political geography, natural resource management, and violent conflicts. He has conducted research in Ghana, Tanzania, Sri Lanka, Ethiopia, and Germany and has also worked as an advisor for international aid agencies, such as the World Bank. Born in southern Germany close to the French border, Dr. Korf lived and worked in Germany until 2005.

DR. ANTJE SCHLOTTMANN is a researcher and lecturer in the field of social geography at the University of Jena, Germany. Her research focuses on regional identity, in particular east, west, and central Germany. Dr. Schlottmann is a regular contributor to educational journals and is active in school and adult education.

Time Line of German History

A.D.

800 Charlemagne is crowned emperor of the Holy Roman Empire in Rome.

962 Otto I is crowned Holy Roman Emperor in Rome and the Byzantine emperor recognizes his title.

1300

1348 The Black Death, a form of plague, sweeps through central Europe, killing many of the population.

1400

1438 The crown of the Holy Roman Empire passes to the Habsburg family; all but one future emperor are Habsburgs.

1455 Johannes Gutenberg prints a Bible in the city of Mainz; it is the first book printed in the West with movable type.

1500

1517 The Protestant Reformation begins in Germany when Martin Luther publishes his 95 Theses, which condemn corruption in the Roman Catholic Church. The Reformation begins centuries of warfare among German states.

1555 The Peace of Augsburg declares that the rulers of German states have the right to dictate whether their subjects should be Protestant or Catholic.

1600

1618 The Thirty Years' War begins with a protest by Bohemian Protestants in Prague.

1648 The Peace of Westphalia ends the Thirty Years' War.

1700

1756 The German state of Prussia begins the Seven Years' War against Austria, France, Russia, Sweden, and other states in the Holy Roman Empire.

1800

1806 Defeat by the French emperor Napoleon ends the Holy Roman Empire. In its place he creates the Confederation of the Rhine.

1815 After two years of warfare, Germany throws off French control.

1815 Prussia, Austria, and Russia form an alliance in an effort to prevent liberal movements calling for political change.

1848 After a series of revolutions in Germany, the Prussian National Assembly creates a constitutional monarchy.

1849 King Frederick William IV is crowned emperor.

1862 Otto von Bismarck becomes prime minister of Prussia.

1866 Prussia and Austria go to war, which leads to the end of the German Confederation.

1871 Prussia leads German states in a victorious war against France; the German Empire is founded with William I as its kaiser (emperor) and Bismarck as its chancellor.

1888 William I dies and is succeeded by Frederick.